This
book
belongs
to:

Scripture verses on pages 3, 47, 69, and 91 are taken from The ESV® Bible (The Holy Bible, English Standard Version®), copyright © 2001 by Crossway, a publishing ministry of Good News Publishers. Used by permission. All rights reserved.

Scripture verses on pages 113, 135, 157 are taken from the Holy Bible, New International Version®, NIV®. Copyright © 1973, 1978, 1984, 2011 by Biblica, Inc.® Used by permission. All rights reserved worldwide.

Cover by Nicole Dougherty

Interior design by Janelle Coury

Ruth Chou Simons is published in association with William K. Jensen Literary Agency, 119 Bampton Court, Eugene, Oregon 97404.

gracelaced journal

Copyright © 2017 by Ruth Chou Simons
Art copyright © 2017 by Ruth Chou Simons
Published by Harvest House Publishers
Eugene, Oregon 97402
www.harvesthousepublishers.com

ISBN 978-0-7369-7211-6 (pbk.)

Printed in China

17 18 19 20 21 22 23 24 25 / RDS-JC / 10 9 8 7 6 5 4 3 2 1

the Lord is near to the brokenhearted and saves the crushed in spirit.

PSALM 34:18

Thou hast made us for Thyself, O Lord, and our heart is restless until it finds its rest in Thee.

AUGUSTINE OF HIPPO

fear not,
for I have
redeemed you;
I have
called you
by name,
you are
mine.

ISAIAH 43:1

for freedom Christ has set us free.

GALATIANS 5:1

let us then with confidence draw near to the throne of grace, THAT WE MAY RECEIVE *mercy* AND *find grace* TO HELP IN *time of need.*

HEBREWS 4:16

But encourage one another daily, as long as it is called today, so that none of you may be hardened by sin's deceitfulness. HEBREWS 3:13

He is before all things and in Him all things

HOLD TOGETHER.

colossians 1:17

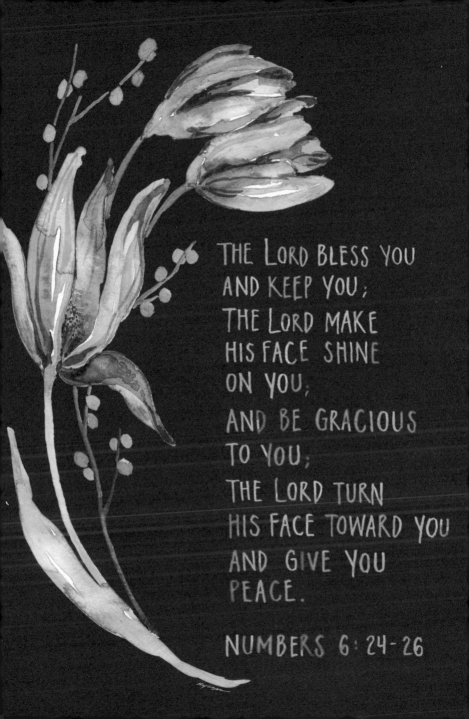

THE LORD BLESS YOU
AND KEEP YOU;
THE LORD MAKE
HIS FACE SHINE
ON YOU;
AND BE GRACIOUS
TO YOU;
THE LORD TURN
HIS FACE TOWARD YOU
AND GIVE YOU
PEACE.

NUMBERS 6:24-26

This Journey Is as Perennial as the Seasons

GraceLaced, the book, is about more than pretty florals and fanciful brushwork—it's about flourishing. With carefully crafted intention, this beautiful volume of seasonal devotions from artist and author Ruth Chou Simons encourages readers in any circumstance to become deeply rooted in God's faithful promises. *GraceLaced* extends a soul-stirring invitation to draw close to God while…

> *resting* in who He is
> *rehearsing* the truth He says about you
> *responding* in faith to those truths
> *remembering* His provision to sustain you, time and time again

Who we are and *who He is* never changes, even though everything else rarely stays the same. Let this book point you to truth as you journey through the changing seasons of your heart.